CHARLES REZNIKOFF

BY MILTON HINDUS

BOOKS BY CHARLES REZNIKOFF

Rhythms, 1918
Rhythms II, 1919
Poems, 1920
Uriel Accosta: A Play & A Fourth Group of Verse, 1921
Chatterton, the Black Death, and Meriwether Lewis, 1922 (plays)
Coral and Captive Israel, 1923 (plays)
Nine Plays, 1927
Five Groups of Verse, 1927
By the Waters of Manhattan: An Annual, 1929 (anthology)
By the Waters of Manhattan, 1930 (novel)
Jerusalem the Golden, 1934
Testimony, 1934 (prose)
In Memoriam: 1933, 1934
Early History of a Sewing Machine Operator (with Nathan Reznikoff), 1936 (prose)
Separate Way, 1936
Going To and Fro and Walking Up and Down, 1941
The Lionhearted, 1944 (novel)
Inscriptions: 1944-1956, 1959
By the Waters of Manhattan: Selected Verse, 1962
Family Chronicle (with Nathan and Sarah Reznikoff), 1963 (prose)
Testimony: The United States 1885-1890: Recitative, 1965
Testimony: The United States (1891-1900): Recitative, 1968
By the Well of Living and Seeing and The Fifth Book of the Maccabees, 1969
By the Well of Living & Seeing: New & Selected Poems 1918-1973, 1974
Holocaust, 1975
Poems 1918-1936: Volume I of the Complete Poems of Charles Reznikoff, 1976

CHARLES REZNIKOFF:

A CRITICAL ESSAY

By

MILTON HINDUS

Santa Barbara
Black Sparrow Press
1977

CHARLES REZNIKOFF: A CRITICAL ESSAY
 For information address Black Sparrow Press, Box 3993, Santa Barbara, CA, 93105.

Cover photograph by Craig Vander Lende.

ISBN 0-87685-365-3 (trade paper edition)
ISBN 0-87685-366-1 (trade cloth edition)

Charles Reznikoff: A Critical Essay

FOR MARIE SYRKIN

"... and the day's brightness dwindles into stars."

THE poet Charles Reznikoff was born in Brooklyn, New York, on August 30, 1894. He died in Manhattan on January 22, 1976. Except for the year (1910-1911) that he spent at the School of Journalism of the University of Missouri and the somewhat longer period in the 1930's in which he worked in Hollywood, he never left New York. He never travelled outside the United States and was very much attached to his native city. He was an early riser and walked many miles in the city streets and parks every day before noon. The delight he found in these walks has left many marks in his poetry and prose. Though he could hardly be described as a programmatic "city poet" or "New York poet," he was both of these, among other things, and he found the title "By the Waters of Manhattan," which he first used for a novel in 1930, so representative of his tastes and concerns that he used the same title again early in the 1960's for his volume of selected poems. In his later years, the streets of his city and its parks (like those of other American cities in the same period) became dangerous to pedestrians, and one morning he was "mugged," robbed and seriously hurt while walking on Riverside Drive. But he recovered and resumed those morning walks so important to his life and work. The pleasure he took in the simplest and most ordinary things was palpable to all who knew him and has found embodiment in some of the lyrics and "Images" which were among his earliest publications:

> Feast, you who cross the bridge
> this cold twilight
> on these honeycombs of light, the buildings of Manhattan.

The study of journalism did not hold him for long. Like many modern writers (Joyce, Pound, Proust), he found the spirit of journalism and literature antithetical rather than complementary. The emphasis in journalism on the strange and unusual ran counter to his literary instincts. Asked to explain the difference, he would quote, as a parable, the advice traditionally given by the newspaper editor to a fledgling reporter: "If a dog bites a man, that's no news, but if a man bites a dog, that, son, is news!" Literature, on the other hand, was capable of making something out of nothing; by stressing the inward component of experience, the imagination could render meaningful and even exciting the most commonplace everyday happenings in which nothing of any outward consequence seemed to occur. Not "newspaper news" but the "simple news" that Emily Dickinson found every day in her garden and he found in his city streets was what concerned him. That second kind of "news" which the papers never reported was the kind which might remain news forever.

In 1912, Reznikoff entered the New York University Law School. He found more here than he had previously in journalism. He stayed the course, worked hard for four years, graduated second in his class, and in 1916 was admitted to the bar of the State of New York. Though he practiced only very briefly, the study of the law had a permanent and salutary effect on him, as he tells us in his "Early History of a Writer." From it he acquired the habit of

> prying sentences open to look at the exact meaning:
> weighing words to choose only those that had meat for
>   my purpose
> and throwing the rest away as empty shells.

Studying law helped rid him of complacency about his own writing. He became self-critical, learning painfully to

> . . . scrutinize every word and phrase
> as if in a document or the opinion of a judge
> and listen, as well, for tones and overtones,
> leaving only the pithy, the necessary, the clear and plain.

But the law was more than merely useful to him; it touched his imagination:

> The law that we studied

was not always the actual law
of judges or statutes
but an ideal—
from which new branches were ever springing
as society became complicated
and the new rights of its individuals clear.
I found it delightful
to climb those green heights,
to bathe in the clear waters of reason,
to use words for their daylight meaning
and not as prisms
playing with the rainbows of connotations . . .

Reacting against romanticism (like much of his generation), excess, symbolism, obscurity, he found he loved almost as much as the streets:

the plain sunlight of the cases,
the sharp prose,
the forthright speech of the judges;
it was good, too, to stick my mind against the sentences
of a judge,
and drag the meaning out of the shell of words.

The law as an ideal may even have merged at times with what he took to be the central meaning of his Jewish heritage, as one may see in the eloquent conclusion of his little playlet "Rashi":

Jacob is like the stars
Which rise to their station,
Which the winds cannot blow away
Nor clouds extinguish.
But we become names upon gravestones and upon books,
Our desire for the law an inheritance
Among our grandsons.
It was good to labor, and after labor
It is good to rest.

Yet the law was not really the vocation of Reznikoff any more than journalism had been. Every man is "large" (to use

Whitman's word); he "contains multitudes." I did not learn until after Reznikoff's death that in his youth he had apparently considered the idea of taking a doctorate in history and becoming a professional historian. If he did not realize this ambition, he still managed to do work which professional historians could respect. He translated a history written in German: I. J. Benjamin's *My Three Years in the United States: 1859-1862.* With the assistance of Uriah Engelman, he wrote a history of the Jews of Charleston, South Carolina, sound enough to be cited even now as a model of its kind. He edited, in two volumes, the public papers of Louis Marshall (who was a serious candidate for an appointment to the United States Supreme Court before Louis D. Brandeis was chosen). He wrote a viable historical novel about medieval England, *The Lionhearted.* He made use of historical materials in his little book *Nine Plays,* which gave us glimpses of such personages as Thomas Chatterton, Uriel Acosta, the medieval Jewish scholar Rashi, Meriwether Lewis, and others. As early as 1934, he combined his interest in history and in the law to produce a volume of vignettes (as Kenneth Burke described them) of life in the various sections of the United States in earlier times drawn from the volumes of law reports which he worked on while employed by the firm publishing *Corpus Juris,* described as an encyclopaedia of law for lawyers. Like Frost, he thus managed to unite his avocation with his vocation. He called this crossing of history and law *Testimony* and used the same title for the volumes he added in the 1960's, which were concerned with the sectional life of the United States between 1885 and 1915. The form of verse which he developed for this task he called "recitative." The 1930 novel *By the Waters of Manhattan* was concerned with the life of the Jewish immigrants of New York in the late nineteenth century, his father's generation; so was his autobiographical *Family Chronicle,* consisting of the "Early History of a Seamstress" (about his mother, Sarah Reznikoff), the "Early History of a Sewing-Machine Operator" (about his father, Nathan Reznikoff), and "Needle Trade" (about his own experience while working as a salesman in the business owned by his parents during the 1920's).

In "Tradition and the Individual Talent," Eliot tells us that what he calls "the historical sense [is] nearly indispensable to anyone who would continue to be a poet beyond his twenty-fifth year." Reznikoff had no difficulty in this respect, since he seems to have been born with such a historical sense. He may have owed some of that to the fact that he was born a member of an ancient people for whom (to use Stephen Dedalus's description, drawn from his own experience) history was a nightmare from which it was vain to try to awaken. The consciousness of this common bond may have been what drew Reznikoff to use Joyce's *Portrait of the Artist* as the model for his own novel *By the Waters of Manhattan.* This succeeded an "Imagist" phase in which his acknowledged model was Pound. There is a vein of profound pessimism expressed in Reznikoff's refrain in one of his poems: "We go our separate ways to death." He has a morbid vision of individuals as well as whole societies plunging as if through a trapdoor into "the dark backward and abysm of time." The fascination of history is precisely that of fathoming imaginatively the unfathomable retrospect of an endless past.

We all belong to history, but we do not all know it. And even those who glimpse this truth may do so intermittently. We tend to think of History (with a capital) as consisting of privileged moments in the lives of privileged people. As the cynic put it, Roman real estate transactions are not regarded generally as part of history, but when they are those of Caesar they are history. Coming into contact with what one recognizes to be history in the high sense of the term can be an unnerving experience, which inspires to expression those who might otherwise be counted among the voiceless tribes. Survivors of great events and disasters, shipwrecks, wars, concentration camps, like those people whom chance or opportunity has brought into contact with kings or presidents of great countries or other presumable "leaders of the people," often feel compelled to record their experience in some form with the absolute conviction that it may be of some use and interest to antiquarians, scholars, historians, their own descendants, and perhaps even general readers gifted with exceptional curiosity. The writers of such documents (which, however unrefined, are not unreal or unreadable) often seem to be in the grip of a compulsion like that of Coleridge's ancient mariner whose heart, we recall, "within him burned" until his tale was told. The spell holds the reader as it did the writer.

Much rarer, more subtle and sophisticated is a feeling like Reznikoff's that everything that has happened anywhere to anyone is part and parcel of history and would be deserving of attention if it were adequately related. This anti-elitist conception is Whitman's and Tolstoy's. It is that of the Sicilian Prince di Lampedusa, author of *The Leopard,* who recorded his conviction in his autobiographical "Places of My Infancy," that "there are no memoirs, even those written by insignificant people, which do not include social and graphic details of first-rate importance." Gertrude Stein is one of those who experienced the feeling powerfully, which is why she entitled the sequel to her celebrated *Autobiography of Alice B. Toklas, Everybody's Autobiography.* In her huge, supposedly unreadable book *The Making of Americans* (unreadable is the way Edmund Wilson describes it), she is insistent on the inescapable importance of her story of the immigrant experience of a family like her own. "This is not just an ordinary kind of novel with a plot and conversations to amuse you," she writes, "but a record of a decent family. . . . So listen while I tell you all about us, and wait while I hasten slowly forwards, and love, please, this history of this decent family's progress. . . ."

It would be erroneous, I think, to regard such a statement as ironic. It could have described her impression of such a classic document of immigrant autobiography as the one which may have inspired both her title and her book: Jacob Riis's *The Making of an American.* It might also describe Reznikoff's *Family Chronicle.* He is confident of the importance of his material, which he presents in a studiedly non-journalistic, anti-melodramatic manner, and he is concerned lest the impatient reader (as he calls him) miss the significance of such a record as he is making. But he refuses to tone up or trick out the material in any way calculated to win reluctant attention. His presentation is always on a level with his ordinary, unsensational material. It is a harder feat than may be imagined. And in the end it gives the book a claim to preservation as a sort of secular scripture. It is far removed from what Whitman once called "those rivers and oceans of very readable print" (newspapers, magazines, popular books) which make no claim, as literature does, to being more than ephemeral. Though an egalitarian, he cannot deny the immense distinction between the daily "manna" of news meant to satisfy the appetites of the public and the "news that stays news" and is literature.

Reznikoff's poetry, when it is not "recitative" (a kind of half-way house to prose), is melodic language, charged with meaning to the utmost degree. His lyrics are distinguished by the most careful, painstaking verbal craftsmanship. He is a stylist in the sense that he chooses each of his words with precision and sets it with meticulous attention in its place in the sentence. At his best, he is capable of creating little artifacts out of words of jewel-like perfection not unworthy of comparison with the inscriptions and epigrams conserved in the Classic anthologies. That he recognized this affinity is suggested by the title *Inscriptions,* which he gave to one of his slender, privately printed collections. His taste is indicated by the Latin epigram from Martial which served him as the epigraph both for his volume *Jerusalem, the Golden* and his book of selected poems, *By the Waters of Manhattan.* His quest for brevity and point also made him take pleasure (like Pound and other Imagists) in the extreme condensation of such forms of Oriental poetry as the Japanese *haiku.* One of his intricate inventions he titles:

Te Deum

Not because of victories
I sing,
having none,
but for the common sunshine,
the breeze,
the largess of the spring.

Not for victory
but for the day's work done
as well as I was able;
not for a seat upon the dais
but at the common table.

It repays one to read over and over again this "simple" construction. The contrast between the Latin (hymn) title and the meaning of the rest of the poem is striking. Less striking is the patterning of the rhymes: victories/breeze; sing/spring; none/

done; able/table. Only the tonic quality of the closing one is readily noticeable; the rest are all skillfully understated and worked in seemingly by the way. Then there are the alliterations (sing/sunshine/spring/seat) and the assonances (the echoing, for example, of the word *day* in line 8 by the word *dais* in line 10, and the succession of long *a* sounds in four successive lines, 8 through 11). The parallelism of grammatical construction (Not . . . but), important to the theme, is repeated three times: once in the first stanza and twice in the shorter second stanza. An epic note appears in the line "I sing," which echoes both the title and Virgil. The abstemiousness with regard to the adjectives (these come down to the single word *common,* twice used) is compensated for by the felicitous choice of the noun *largess* to describe the bounty of spring.

But what makes the verses really memorable (irregular though they are, according to strict metronomic notions and traditional expectations) is not the technical expertise alone but the "message," the solid democratic sense of it. Reznikoff celebrates the individual rather than social man and also the freedom to be found in a non-competitive enjoyment of the simple life. It is less surprising, in the light of this, that a younger generation which had learned to prize similar qualities should have found him out late in his life. As we turn this many-faceted poem about, we may discover other meanings in it, too. We may find, for example, the pathos of that moment of acute self-awareness which comes when one has been placed by the world (for mysterious reasons which only the world knows) in a position somewhere "below the salt." The persona of this poem is identical with the ironically designated "nobody" in Emily Dickinson's lyric: "I'm nobody! Who are you?" Somehow the suggestion is subtly insinuated that the unobtrusive "able" man seated at "the common table" may be worth more in human terms than many on the "dais" who have been impressed with their own elevation and are busily announcing their names to all in the hoarse tone of Miss Dickinson's frog.

Reznikoff obviously enjoys his own ability to boil down a mass of material into its concentrated essence. See, for example, what he has made of a parable we have all learned in school as children:

The nail is lost. Perhaps the shoe;
horse and rider, kingdom, too.

Told this way, the old worn-down tale achieves a new brightness. It reminds us of an original which has indelibly impressed itself on our memory for no better reason than the oft-cited:

Thirty days hath September
April, June, and November.

The triviality of the rhyme mocks itself slyly and may even mock the importance attached by conventional rhymesters to "the jingle of like endings." The introduction of the single word *perhaps* serves to bring into the open universe of chances the closed and frightening world imposed on the child's imagination by the cautionary original: "For want of a nail, the shoe was lost; for want of a shoe, the horse was lost; for want of a horse, the rider was lost; for want of a rider, the kingdom was lost!" We never realized perhaps how stifling this notion of necessity was. Reznikoff takes just fifteen syllables to free our mind.

The shy and hidden humor in this couplet is more marked elsewhere. It is a humor reserved and personal in quality and somewhat dry, though it is not incapable, as C. P. Snow noted, of shading into sarcasm.

Fraser, I think, tells of a Roman
who loved a tree in his garden so much
he would kiss and embrace it.

This is going pretty far
even for a lover of nature
and I do not think it would be allowed
in Central Park.

The same quality of wit is present in some of what he chooses to call his *Glosses* (this one on a Biblical text):

As I sit in the street-car and hear the chatter about me,
I do not envy Solomon
who understood the language of birds as well.

What do the birds talk about?
The weather, I suppose.
O yes, they brought Solomon news
of what was said about him
so that it became a proverb not to speak of the king,
even in one's bedroom, lest a bird tell it.

Occasionally, a poem in two lines approaches the pointedness of a Roman epigram:

Of our visitors—I do not know which I dislike most:
the silent beetles or these noisy flies.

Sometimes he almost seems to be translating the verses of a satirist complaining about the traffic problems and congestion (not so different from our own) in ancient Rome:

Permit me to warn you
against this automobile rushing to embrace you
with outstretched fender.

Urban subjects, like subways and graffiti, are natural for his delicate humor:

This subway station
with its electric lights, pillars of steel, arches
  of cement, and trains—
quite an improvement on the caves of the cavemen;
but, look! on this wall
a primitive drawing.

When his verses are less "pointed," they are often brilliant Imagist observations of the kind one finds in the earlier poetry of William Carlos Williams:

About an excavation
a flock of bright red lanterns
has settled.

Another example:

The cat in our neighbor's yard has convulsions:
from her mouth a green jet on the pavement—
she has added a leaf to their garden.

Reznikoff was born nine years after Ezra Pound and has obviously owed much to the example of the older poet for whose technical abilities he expressed a continuing admiration. In 1914 when Reznikoff was twenty years old, a perhaps especially impressionable age aesthetically speaking, Pound made his statement: "The point of Imagism is that it does not use images as *ornaments*. The image itself is the speech." From this point on, according to literary historians, for poets influenced by his theory, images rather than abstract or general statements became "the fundamental building blocks of poetry." By his practice, Reznikoff has demonstrated how well he learned the lesson which Pound expressed when he said, in an oft-quoted definition, "An 'image' is that which presents an intellectual and emotional complex in an instant of time." The guiding maxim of his work might equally well have been supplied by Amy Lowell when she declared in her Imagist manifesto that appeared in an anthology which she published in 1915: "Concentration is the very essence of poetry."

It is interesting to observe the process by which Reznikoff boils down a mass of prosaic material presented in a plain style into one of his characteristic couplets, laconic and often stinging. One of the cases Reznikoff discovered in the law reports he was working on he described in the following lines:

Amelia was just fourteen and out of the orphan asylum;
at her first job—in the factory, and yes sir,
yes madam, oh, so anxious to please.
She stood at the table, her blonde hair hanging about
her shoulders, "knocking up" for Mary and Sadie,
the stitchers
("knocking up" is counting books and stacking them in
piles to be taken away).
There were twenty wire-stitching machines on the floor,
worked by a shaft that ran under the table,
as each stitcher put her work through the machine,
she threw it on the table. The books were piling up fast

and some slid to the floor
(the forelady had said, Keep the work off the floor!);
three or four had fallen under the table
between the boards nailed against the legs.
She felt her hair caught gently;
put her hand up and felt the shaft going round and round
and her hair caught on it, wound and winding around it,
until the scalp was jerked from her head,
and the blood was coming down all over face and waist.

The material of this horrifying episode of American industrial history appears to have been subsequently distilled by the poet into two striking lines on another subject altogether:

My hair was caught in the wheels of a clock
and torn from my head: see, I am bald!

In its raw state, the content of *Testimony* resembles that of the so-called proletarian writers; the difference between Reznikoff and the "proletarians" is that his aesthetic conscience is as watchful as that of James Joyce. His interest in communicating his compassion never takes precedence over his concern with style, with words, with experimentation. The case-history, however heart-rending, is less important than his never ending search for concentration and distinction. His compassion never becomes sentimental or maudlin; the tears are dried out by his humor, which instead of undermining the authenticity of his feeling strengthens it. Here, for example, is his picture of "an elevator operator" (in the days before he was made obsolete by automation):

The elevator man, working long hours
for little—whose work is dull and trivial—
must also greet each passenger
pleasantly:
to be so heroic
he wears a uniform.

And here is a vignette entitled "Scrubwoman":

One shoulder lower,
with unsure steps like a bear erect,
the smell of the wet black rags that she cleans
with about her.

Scratching with four stiff fingers her half-bald head,
smiling.

His portraits of immigrants belong to the same category of the pitiable who are presented with restraint and understatement:

She sat by the window opening into the airshaft,
and looking across the parapet
at the new moon.

She would have taken the hairpins out of her
carefully coiled hair,
and thrown herself on the bed in tears;
but he was coming and her mouth had to be pinned
into a smile.
If he would have her, she would marry him whatever he was.

A knock. She lit the gas and opened her door.
Her aunt and the man—skin loose under his eyes,
face slashed with wrinkles.
"Come in," she said as gently as she could and smiled.

Here is how he depicts a "Ghetto Funeral":

Followed by his lodge, shabby men stumbling
over cobblestones,
and his children, faces red and ugly with tears,
eyes and eyelids red,
in the black coffin in the black hearse the old man.

No longer secretly grieving
that his children are not strong enough to go the
way he wanted to go
and was not strong enough.

Reznikoff's religious sentiments, which are unmistakably present in many of his poems (this presence, too, serves to separate him from the "proletarians"), are difficult to define precisely. His God, except in direct translations from the Bible, is perhaps nearer to the God of Spinoza and of Whitman than He is to the God of Jewish tradition, as is evident in these lines:

> Out of nothing I became a being,
> and from a being I shall be
> nothing—but until then
> I rejoice, a mote in Your world,
> a spark in Your seeing.

A more personal expression of faith is to be found in seven lines in which Reznikoff speaks of the significance of his given names in English and in Hebrew:

> Because, the first-born, I was not redeemed,
> I belong to my Lord, not to myself or you:
> by my name, in English, I am of His house,
> one of the carles—a Charles, a churl;
> and by my name in Hebrew which is Ezekiel
> (Whom God strengthened)
> my strength, such as it is, is His.

These learned lines require commentary. The compressed opening:

> Because, the first-born, I was not redeemed,
> I belong to my Lord . . .

refers to the Jewish custom of redeeming (or ransoming) the first-born son of the family, a custom which originates in a number of verses in the Bible (*Exodus* 13:13 and 34:20; *Numbers* 3:11, 46ff. and 18:15-16). The initial impulse of the poem may have come from chapter 13 of *Exodus*:

> And the Lord spoke unto Moses, saying: "Sanctify unto Me all the first-born, whatsoever openeth the womb among

> the children of Israel, both of man and of beast, it is Mine." And Moses said unto the people: "Remember this day, in which ye came out from Egypt, out of the house of bondage; for by strength of hand the Lord brought you out from this place. . . . And every firstling of an ass thou shalt redeem with a lamb; and if thou wilt not redeem it, then thou shalt break its neck; and all the first-born of man among thy sons shalt thou redeem. And it shall be when thy son asketh them in time to come, saying: What is this? that thou shalt say unto him: By strength of hand the Lord brought us out from Egypt, from the house of bondage; And it came to pass, when Pharaoh would hardly let us go, that the Lord slew all the first-born in the land of Egypt, both the first-born of man, and the first-born of beast; therefore I sacrifice to the Lord all that openeth the womb, being males; *but all the first-born of my sons I redeem . . .*"

The gnarled and somewhat shamefaced or at least reticent opening words of the poem would seem to indicate that in the Reznikoff household the ancient custom of redeeming the first-born son was "honored in the breach rather than the observance." Going on to the third and fourth lines, the English name *Charles* is derived by the lexicon from an ancient word meaning man or male. The German word *kerl* is also behind the word *churl*, meaning bondsman originally, villein or serf. The name *Charles*, of course, has a royal sound to English ears, and it is ironic, therefore, that it should derive from such humble connections. The royalty of the name *Charles*, however, may have suggested the kingship of God, whose bondsman the writer is. The concluding lines on the derivation of the Hebrew name *Ezekiel* are self-explanatory. What may require some explanation, however, is the leap that brings us from the Hebrew *Ezekiel* to the English name *Charles*. There would seem to be no connection between the two, yet the association may not be as arbitrary as it looks. Boys named Ezekiel were generally called *Chatzkl* in Yiddish, an abbreviation which might suggest *Charles*, a name which no doubt rang with aristocratic overtones in immigrant ears. To the poet, on the other hand, it suggested the churl as well as the king, and he assimilates its implications, therefore, to his prevailing democratic theme. He is strengthened by God precisely because he is one of the common people whom God especially loves.

Let us turn our attention now to a passage from a longer poem:

> Out of the strong, sweetness;
> and out of the dead body of the lion of Judah,
> the prophecies and psalms;
> out of the slaves in Egypt,
> out of the wandering tribesmen of the deserts
> and the peasants of Palestine,
> out of the slaves of Babylon and Rome,
> out of the ghettos of Spain and Portugal, Germany and
> Poland
> the Torah and the prophecies,
> the Talmud and the sacred studies, the hymns and songs
> of the Jews;
> and out of the Jewish dead
> of Belgium and Holland, of Rumania, Hungary, and
> Bulgaria,
> of France and Italy and Yugoslavia,
> of Lithuania and Latvia, White Russia and Ukrainia,
> of Czechoslovakia and Austria,
> Poland and Germany,
> out of the greatly wronged
> a people teaching and doing justice;
> out of the plundered
> a generous people;
> out of the wounded a people of physicians;
> and out of those who met only with hate,
> a people of love, a compassionate people.

In these Whitmanian lines, what pitfalls of sentimentality for the unwary writer have been successfully skirted thanks to Reznikoff's unfailing tact. He is able to avoid the high-pitched false note with the sure-footedness of a sleepwalker on the edge of an abyss.

Ethnic affiliation in a writer, ideally speaking, should be as unobtrusive as the bond watermark in paper, becoming visible only when held up to the light of analysis. A writer at ease with his own identity may range in his expression of it from the most intense pride in his national heritage to mockery and criticism which hovers at times on the dangerous edge of "self-hatred." When a people's fortunes are in the ascendant and they are supremely confident of their future, the expression of a writer's variable feelings toward it, no matter how unflattering, can be good-humoredly accepted by it. Shakespeare can traverse the gamut from the passionate patriotism of York's speech about England in *Richard II* to the sly and sarcastic digs at English gullibility and foolishness in *The Tempest* and in *Hamlet* and make his countrymen either glow with self-approval or laugh heartily at their own foibles and shortcomings. Even a chauvinistic Slavophil like Dostoyevsky permits himself the freedom occasionally to poke fun at his fellow-Russians. Whitman the nationalist was brutally frank about the corruption of America in the Gilded Age in the indictment which he called *Democratic Vistas.* And though no one was attached to ancient Athens more than Socrates, his stinging criticisms of its democratic polity made many of the citizens suspect him of harboring sympathies for her authoritarian rival Sparta.

Among the Jewish people in its greatest ancient period, the ambivalence of the relation between it and its greatest prophetic sons, beginning with Moses, is clearly set forth in the Bible. In modern times, during the long ages of Jewish dispersion among the other peoples of the earth with its attendant periodic persecutions and pogroms, emotions have become ever more complicated and contradictory and their expression more problematical and beset with extreme difficulties. The result has been that Jewish writers who have succeeded in satisfying "the world" have rarely satisfied their fellow-Jews and that those who have pleased their fellow-Jews have gained little general approbation among others. Reznikoff belongs to the second of these categories. Despite the "non-sectarian" appreciation he has received now and then, he is generally regarded, when he is known at all, as "a literary Jew."

Yet it is a mistake to regard him as one-sided. He made a lifelong literary effort to harmonize the born American in himself with the Jew deeply loyal to his Jewish heritage. He is not among those writers who have striven to suppress one or another of these motivations and have sometimes succeeded only in falling between two stools. In his work, both the American and the Jew are present and move harmoniously together. Very early in his literary life, he seems to have made a resolution somewhat similar to the one which Stephen Dedalus expressed in Joyce's *Portrait of the Artist as a Young Man*: "This [Jewish] race and this country [America] and this [American Jewish] life produced me. . . . I shall express myself as I am!" Reznikoff is remarkable in the unselfconscious naturalness of the relationship he has achieved between his disparate elements. He indulges in no heroics or sentimentality. He is neither apologetic nor self-deprecating. He somehow succeeded in bypassing most of the tensions, temptations and dilemmas of allegiance that are the rule rather than the exception among the Jewish writers of America in our time. What safeguarded his tranquility most effectively perhaps is that Reznikoff belonged to the category of writers for whom art could never become a mere adjective rather than a noun with a capital letter. While Imagists like Pound and "proletarians" like Michael Gold were threatening at times to disappear down the vortex of opposing extreme ideologies, Reznikoff hewed patiently to the initial aesthetic course he had embarked on. Stanislaus Joyce once told how his brother James had interrupted him as he was talking about Italian Fascism with the impatient remark: "Don't speak to me about politics! I'm interested only in style!" It is some such attitude that also sheltered Reznikoff and saved him from the loss of faith in the validity of his literary vocation suffered by so many writers of his generation.

Testimony proposed to describe impressionistically the life of various sections of the United States in earlier periods: "The South," "The North" and "The West." These large sections are subdivided by the author under such headings as "Domestic Scenes," Property," "Chinese" (in the section on the West), "Negroes" both in the South and in the North), "Railroads," "Machine Age," etc. Jews as such, in the early sections, are not identified and never become prominent. One selection appears to deal with a Jew named Rosenzweig who is a travelling salesman. The incident recounted is a sadistic one in which a mean conductor orders Rosenzweig off the train in the middle of nowhere late at night because he has somehow gotten the wrong ticket. No argument by the poor man, no pleading or offer to pay for his passage softens the heart of the conductor, and the salesman after being forced to get off wanders around in a daze among the dark tracks of a complicated railroad junction until he is finally struck from behind by a locomotive. The reader assumes that Reznikoff found this incident recorded in the transcript of a suit for damages against the railroad by the man's survivors. No trace or hint of a motivation for the conductor's cruelty appears in the "Objectivist" treatment of the scene. It is possible that anti-Semitism is involved, but we cannot be sure. In any case, the cruelty is not exceptional. Over and over again in these pages man's inhumanity to man (of which the Holocaust is history's quintessential example) is illustrated. The weak and the helpless in these pages attract the sadistic and the evil like magnets. Animals, children, the sick, the ignorant, women, minorities of various kinds, are the favorite victims. The cruelty may be purposeful, but just as often it may exist for its own sake (like art) and appease some incurably corrupt and vicious streak in human nature itself. Here is a typical passage of "recitative" in *Testimony*:

> Tilda was just a child
> when she began to work for the Tells.
> Her mother was dead
> and her father had given up their home.
> When, as is the way with women,
> her monthly sickness first began,
> she was frightened
> and told Mrs. Tell about it:
> "That is bad," the farmer's wife said
> "and dangerous:
> you might go crazy and die.
> There is only one thing to do:
> work hard!
> Work as hard as you can,
> and you may still get well!"
>
> She was up at five in the morning
> and on her feet until ten or eleven at night:
> milked fourteen cows daily;

carried water uphill
for forty head of hogs; dug and brought potatoes
from the field;
and helped cook for a family of eight;
scrubbed the floors
and took care of the little ones—
did the work
two stout girls had done.

Reznikoff chose a passage from Paul's *Epistle to the Ephesians* as the overall epigraph of *Testimony.* A passage from Pound's *Guide to Kulchur* seems to me to describe Reznikoff's intent very well: "The records of rascality (as conserved in fragments of law records) are so good one grudges them to the prose page, and wants to reserve them for poetry." Also apt as a description of the evil and chicanery that are revealed in these pages is a passage that occurs in Whitman's conversations with Horace Traubel: "Oh the human being is a bad critter: as the old Emperor Frederick would say, we're a bad lot—a bad lot, taken all in all."

A legitimate objection may be raised against Reznikoff's idea of deriving the colors of his palette for painting a picture of life in the United States during a certain period at the end of the nineteenth and the beginning of the twentieth centuries from cases that had to be settled in the courts. One may argue that these are necessarily extreme cases and that life in general at the time must have been much more benign than the life he chooses to write about. Life as always everywhere, in addition to the sensational events which are the stuff of newspapers and receive the attention of the magistrates, must have contained innumerable instances of generosity, kindness and mutual aid. The objection is similar to the one that Prince Kropotkin in his book entitled *Mutual Aid* makes against the ordinary writing of history which he indicts on the grounds of its distortion, partiality and falsification or, at any rate, failure to relate the whole truth about human life.

The objection may be answered in one of two ways. First, it may be said that Reznikoff chooses his instances more often from civil than from criminal law; the significance of this is that the wrongs he is concerned with, though sometimes involving violence and blood, are more often likely to be ordinary rather than extreme wrongs, wrongs involving exploitation (as in the case of "Tilda") and gullibility. In other words, his cases are more representative of ordinary prosaic "uneventful" life than appears at first glance. The second answer might be to grant the force of the objection but to insist that extreme cases tell us something we need to know about life precisely because they highlight aspects of it that may otherwise be overlooked. Scott Fitzgerald suggests that the higher poetic truth of fiction begins precisely at the point where the writer treats the extreme instance as if it were the most ordinary representative one. That is what he himself does so successfully in *The Great Gatsby* and what Dreiser does in *An American Tragedy* and Dostoyevsky in *Crime and Punishment,* Flaubert in *Madame Bovary,* and Tolstoy in *Anna Karenina.* Murder and suicide are statistically improbable events, but poetry and truth do not always reside in statistics. Extreme cases drawn from court records and newspaper files, though they may remain only remote possibilities so far as the experience of the vast majority of people is concerned, provide the sensitive writer and his reader profound insights into the society capable of producing them.

Reznikoff's *Testimony,* along with its dominantly somber and even tragic tonalities (the vision of human life in it is basically a darkened post-Holocaust one) also has its lighter moments of comic relief. Reznikoff's humor occasionally recalls the vein of the grotesque found in such a poem as "Tract" by William Carlos Willliams. Here, for example, is one of Reznikoff's "snapshots" depicting a foolish and frustrated robber in the old West:

> He entered the store with barley sacks upon his feet
> and a barley sack over his head—
> holes cut in front through which to look—
> and carried a shotgun,
> both barrels loaded with bird shot.
>
> But the barley sack upon one of his feet
> caught on something at the end of the counter;
> the mask became displaced so that he could not see,
> and the gun was jerked from his hand.

Turning our attention from his verse to his prose, let us look first at his book *Family Chronicle*. *Family Chronicle* is a narrative of immigrant Jewish life in America around the turn of the century, but, like Mary Antin's *The Promised Land,* it is almost evenly divided between descriptions of the background of life in "the old country" of eastern Europe (many immigrants for a long time simply called it "home" or "the old home"—which, oddly and coincidentally, is exactly the way in which Hawthorne refers to England!) and descriptions of the early bitter struggles (both economic and spiritual, but economic even more than spiritual) to take root in the alien soil of the United States. *Family Chronicle* is divided into three equal parts: the first an "autobiography" of the mother, Sarah Reznikoff, composed for her by her writer-son in the same way as *The Autobiography of Alice B. Toklas* was written by her friend Gertrude Stein, which is entitled "Early History of a Seamstress"; the second part an "autobiography" of the father, Nathan Reznikoff, entitled "Early History of a Sewing-Machine Operator"; and, finally, an autobiography of the son and writer himself, Charles, which is called "Needle Trade." The epigraph of this "family chronicle" is from *Ecclesiastes*: "Two are better than one . . . For if they fall, the one will lift up his fellow; but woe unto him that is alone when he falleth . . . and a threefold cord is not quickly broken." In these few simple words is contained the basic reason for the strength, tenacity and survival of the family unit as the building block upon which human societies have been founded throughout the ages.

The book is designed to be something like an archeological "dig" in which the quest is for facts about the lives of east European Jewish immigrants which, in something less than a century, have become almost as elusive to their descendants as facts about prehistoric civilizations thousands of years ago. Reznikoff's "dig" preserves all kinds of odd and arresting items, some of them familiar to students of other "digs," some of them unexpected and belonging to this particular one alone. There is the saintly grandfather, for example, who simply could not bring himself to return evil for evil but naturally turned his other cheek to those who smote him, as Christians are instructed to do in their Gospel yet so rarely manage actually to do. There is the expense of buying water from the water-carrier in the *shtetl* which is remembered with a minimum of nostalgia and without a trace of any lachrymose sentimentality. There is the floor of the "living room" of the house in the old country made out of hardened mud. There are the pogroms, of course, but in the length and breadth of all that has been written on this familiar subject there are no pogroms more understated or flattened out than in the pages of Reznikoff. Everything is, as far as possible, *objectified*: thatched roofs, peasants rolling cigarettes, political prisoners being transported to Siberia, unwilling draftees in the army of the Czar, a boy trying to learn to go through the whole day of Yom Kippur without letting a morsel of food or a drop of water pass his lips and finding it a very painful experience indeed.

In the new world, there are endless details of petty business transactions upon which the lives of whole families depended, encounters with radicals, the pride that a boy takes in his father "the foreman of the ship." There are ghost stories from the old country remembered in the new one, stories about visitations from "the other world" (which is simply the world of the dead), the story of a girl who is forced to choose a suitor she does not really prefer because he is the possessor of a thousand rubles, and the story of a legacy which consists of a pair of phylacteries. There are the wonders of "running water" in America, the endless (fifteen-hour and longer) working days, the struggle to learn a little English when one is just too exhausted to study and is tempted to shut the door to the world outside the ken of the Yiddish newspaper; there is the pathos of a servant girl's modest ambition to rise "from the drudgery of housework to the drudgery of the shop." Reznikoff lovingly preserves not only old facts but old words: the word *tuck*, for example, as it was once used in the clothing industry and now described in the unabridged Webster's as "rare," the word *facer* in the sense of a blow in the face, stemming from the sport of boxing and having the meaning by extension of any severe of stunning shock, check or defeat, a word once used more commonly than now but still recognized by the dictionary as "colloquially" acceptable.

In treating these things, Reznikoff consistently plays them down. He subdues all the highlights of his picture and studiously produces a monochromatic effect (like a study by Whistler) which requires the utmost effort of attention from the reader. Reading this book is a salutary form of discipline. It is as if the author, like so many other literary modernists, is saying to his reader: "If you want to read me, you must do so on my terms, not on your own; you must not expect me to meet you half-way or in any respect to make it easy for you to reach me and my meaning." He does this consciously and with confidence based on the intrinsic importance of his material. He seems to have learned the lesson contained in a sentence by the poet Baudelaire written in praise of the then neglected painter Corot: "He knows how to be a colorist within a narrow range of colors." Nothing is harder for the writer than to accomplish such a feat, or for the reader than to appreciate it. It is the kind of thing Gertrude Stein did very well in her first book, *Three Lives,* which gained her a reputation among some writers but had hardly any readers. Literature and art are not always easy to take, especially in our century.

From the beginning of his literary career it should have been clear that Reznikoff would remain primarily an aesthete in his motivation. The ivory tower in which he sought refuge was not perhaps as lofty as those sought by Joyce and Proust, but it was quite sufficient to secure him against the solicitations of the social-minded "proletarians." Some of these recognized his talent, but they soon noticed that his temperament was "cool" and did not in the least resemble that of a firebrand like Michael Gold (who was born in the same year with him, 1894). When Reznikoff's novel *By the Waters of Manhattan* (the same title he was to use later on for a volume of his selected poems) appeared in 1930 (the year of the depression that was also to see the publication of Michael Gold's *Jews Without Money),* Isidor Schneider remarked of it in his review in *The New York Herald-Tribune Books*: "I cannot recall any book that gives so clear, so unemotional a presentation [of Jewish life]." Schneider, himself a writer strongly engaged on the literary left as an editor of *The New Masses,* said this with obvious regret, yet the observation is quite true.

The protagonist of *By the Waters of Manhattan,* Ezekiel (which, we recall, is the Hebrew name of Charles Reznikoff) is as socially abstentionist and stand-offish as Stephen Dedalus (who refused to join his classmates in signing even such an unexceptionably virtuous document as an appeal for universal peace).

Speaking of his hero, Reznikoff writes:

> Some of those he had known at school were Socialists. What good trying to change material conditions if men were still the same? But how can men better their spiritual conditions if they need their time and energy for bread? they would argue. To each his own, he would think; my work is with the spirit of man. He would never say this; they were too clever to let him escape in an ambiguity, like a god in a cloud.

In some ways, Reznikoff's literary form in *By the Waters of Manhattan* seems as simple and primitive as Michael Gold's in *Jews Without Money,* yet there is a world of difference between the two books. Gold is always excitedly speaking at the top of his voice so that he reminds one of a critic's unkind description of Céline's *Mea Culpa* as a little book in which the author seems to be suffering a case of *"spiritual heat-prostration."* Reznikoff, on the contrary, never raises his voice at all. If he has any fault, it is that he sometimes speaks too softly to be heard except by those especially attuned to him. He seems to err on the side of hiding his light under a bushel. That is why masses of readers have never discovered him; his audience consists of sensitive individuals widely scattered. He always strives to be completely calm, as befits a poet who uses for his material, as Wordsworth did, "emotion recollected in tranquility."

The difference between Reznikoff and others expresses itself in his continual effort to replace direct statement with indirect suggestion and expressive imagery which are intended to serve as the symbolic equivalents of the states of mind that he is trying to describe. Like Whitman, he thinks it is the task of the artist *to picture* rather than to theorize or generalize or explain. In Gold's *Jews Without Money,* the protagonist calls himself "a lonely suicidal boy," but this abstract statement is hardly as effective as the passage in which Reznikoff communicates the very similar feelings of his hero Ezekiel by means of a more potent literary strategy:

> He was tired as if his muscles were tired. If the grave were open, he would step in to be out of the noise of the world

> and its lights, the great light and the lesser light and the many tiny lights that man has made, to rest in the darkness, in the black nothingness for ever. The wind blew dust upon his lips. How should he escape? From how many windows and roofs to fall, before how many trains, cars and motor cars to jump, how easy to walk into the Harlem River, the East River, the Hudson River, the Bay, the Sound, the sea at a hundred beaches.

Reznikoff avoids abstraction as much as possible in favor of graphically illustrating his meaning. He does not *say* outright that his poverty-stricken hero is hungry for food; he *shows* him standing before the windows of a Horn and Hardart Automat. Entering it, the famished Ezekiel

> delighted in the cool water and the rough clean towels. Then he made the rounds of the little compartments and studied through the thick glass the little pots of dark brown beans, the meat pies—the brown crust curling away from the thick dishes—dishes of macaroni with yellow nuggets of melted cheese, the pompous apple dumplings in ermine of vanilla sauce, then the sandwiches: rows bright with sliced tomatoes and green lettuce, with the red of smoked meats, or the pastel tints of cheese.

The sensuousness of such descriptions almost reminds one of Proust, but in Proust the metaphorical descriptions of food seem to arise from the surfeit of a very comfortable society while here we feel that a similar effect springs from the conditions of deprivation of the underprivileged characters that Reznikoff depicts.

It is always the sensitive observer, unaffectedly enjoying his own sense of the world's variety of tactile surfaces, who seems to be at the center of Reznikoff's consciousness. Like the poet Rimbaud, whose visionary eyes transmuted the prosaic brick factories that surround him into delicate-looking mosques, Reznikoff's hallucinating hero in the ugliest sections of New York City "walked along the streets imagining them canals and bathing in their silence." Such a Venice or Amsterdam of the mind became his escape-hatch into beauty from the intolerable pressures which he felt upon him when, late at night, "his mother and sister would still be up. The kitchen in which he slept would be crowded with their talk—to fall on his mind like handfuls of gravel on a pane of glass." The words are Reznikoff's, but the tone, rhythms, imagery are akin to those of Stephen Dedalus, who also sought refuge in pure aestheticism from the mean lower-middle-class surroundings of his home in Dublin. Under the scrutiny of Ezekiel's poetic eyes, even such a humdrum fact of New York life as Central Park magically turns into "a reservoir of trees, bushes and grass."

Reznikoff is aware of the social problem just as the "proletarians" are, but he feels under no obligation as a writer to try to solve it. Awareness begins with Ezekiel's reconstruction of what life in the old world must have been like for his parents. There, one person used to inquire of another: "Why should you want to go to America? Who goes there but bankrupts, embezzlers, and those who have wrecked their lives here?" What changed the minds of such complacent people finally were the recurrent pogroms in Russia which accompanied its social upheavals in the late nineteenth century.

After three weeks of tossing in steerage on the Atlantic, new immigrants arrived in their new home "by the waters of Manhattan" only to be told by earlier Jewish settlers: "The first thing to learn in America is that you can do anything. You will learn. The first thing to do is to try." Others reassure them: "Don't worry about how you are going to get on here. America is a mother: she feeds you and clothes you and helps you in everything." Despite such cheering words, however, Ezekiel's family arrives in New York just as the country is experiencing one of its periodic depressions. The mother, Sarah Yetta, is told by her friends: "America is a blessed land, a land of great plenty. But it is not regulated yet. The people have poured into this country from Europe and some have too much and some not enough."

Exactly how ill-regulated and contradictory American society is, becomes clear from Reznikoff's charming parody of the Horatio Alger success-story. Ezekiel tries to become an entrepreneur by opening a small bookshop on pure speculation. He is literally without a penny to his name. Though born in this country, he seems worse off than Cahan's character David Levinsky, who had landed in Ellis Island in 1885 with four cents in his pocket (that is to say, I suppose, *without a nickel*). Now such a situation might act as a goad and a challenge to a certain kind of man. Theodore Dreiser's financier Cowperwood shows a talent for economic manipulation as a small boy, but Reznikoff's Ezekiel either has no talents at all in this direction or else his talents are precisely the reverse of those of Cowperwood. He is like a creature born to fly who has to make his way through mud! He makes an attempt to stock his new "shop" with books supplied free of charge on a commission basis by publishers who should, according to his way of thinking, welcome the opportunity of backing his venture. Unfortunately, Ezekiel's demeanor and language are not such as to command the kind of confidence necessary to induce them to take a risk. The larger and more reputable publishing houses will have nothing to do with his harebrained scheme. As a businessman, Ezekiel may be compared to Sholom Aleichem's stock-market "plunger" Menachem Mendel; both are *luftmenschen* living more in imagination than in the world of reality. It is clear to everyone but themselves that their grandiose schemes are destined to come to nothing. They are would-be tycoons who are really no more than *schlemiehls*. The only publisher whom Ezekiel is able to interest in his plans is one of the smallest, a hole-in-the-wall businessman himself whose books are rotting away on his warehouse shelves for lack of public demand. Ezekiel examines this operator's catalogue, and his noncommercial heart is naively delighted with the beautiful titles he finds there. "What excellent books you have!" he enthusiastically exclaims, but the publisher hardly appreciates his compliment and replies with the bitter humor of the unsuccessful: "If they were not so good, they might sell!"

Ezekiel knows poverty as familiarly as do the characters of Michael Gold or any "proletarian." Reznikoff writes:

> To pass the time he wondered what he would do if he had a nickel. He might buy a cup of coffee or a bar of chocolate or a box of crackers or a roll and two penny packages of chocolate or an apple and a roll or a loaf of bread. It was ridiculous to be in want of just a nickel in the streets of New York. When he was a boy, he sometimes found a penny—once a dime—in the streets. Surely there were hun-

> dreds and hundreds of dollars in change lying that moment along the miles of sidewalks and in the gutters. If he were to devote himself to looking for it, he might make a good living and, certainly, it was not as unpleasant as some work. He would be in the open air, at least.

In spite of such incitements to resentment and radicalism, Ezekiel is too much of an individual, too conscious of his literary vocation, and too sceptical of the allurements of any social change theory to join his friends whose object is to change the world.

The real difference between the old country and the new is, for Reznikoff, not primarily one of material well-being. To be poor is as hard in America as it was in Russia or Poland, perhaps even harder since it is regarded as somewhat unusual and blame-worthy. Statistics may prove that more Jews have escaped from poverty in the United States than was the case in Czarist Russia, but that is cold comfort to one who, in the midst of the widespread affluence of his co-religionists, has succeeded somehow only in remaining poor. The main difference between America and Russia has to be sought elsewhere than in the economic area. The word *freedom* turns out to be something better than mere cant. There is no one so poor or obscure in America as to lack completely the opportunity of expressing his thought openly to the world. Grandfather Ezekiel in Russia had been something of a poet, as his grandson in America was to be later on, and while travelling around the countryside like Sholom Aleichem's Tevya peddling his wares, he had composed a bundle of verses, but when these were discovered by his widow after his death she had decided to burn them, for they might contain subversive or dangerous thoughts which might get the whole family in trouble with the police. Grandfather Ezekiel's sufferings were destined to be swallowed up in silence. So far as the world was concerned, he would always remain, to use Whitman's word, a "gawk." But the tongue that had been tied by tyranny in Grandfather Ezekiel's mouth began to be loosened in the mouth of his poetic grandson in America who was no more prosperous than his grandfather. Surely such freedom of expression in America is no small thing except perhaps to one who never knew what it was not to have it.

The care with which Reznikoff's words are crocheted together in his prose is as painstaking as in his poetry. In his historical novel *The Lionhearted* (which is about the Jews in medieval England who evidently deserved this description, according to Reznikoff, much more than King Richard, to whom it was applied) the distinction of its style is more impressive than its handling of plot or drawing of characters. In the following passage, for example, a twelfth-century Norman nobleman is speaking to a young Jewish friend in the period preceding the expulsion of the Jews from England:

> The Jews, even if none of you could ever hope to write a chanson like that about Roland, or songs as good as those of Guilhem or Poitiers, have a knack for words, the least and worst of you. Now I know only French. That is enough for me. Let the priest speak Latin and my serf Saxon. When they want me to understand they must speak French. But you, or your father, or your cousins, must know the churl's Saxon if he is to fee you for your medicine; must understand my French if I am to buy your furs and spice; why you must understand Latin to dispute my priest; and Greek and Arabic to read your books of medicine; and, of course, Hebrew to talk among yourselves or to your God. If you are driven out of France, as Philip Augustus has just driven you out of Paris, or you are banished from Germany, say, to the land of the Polacks—you must set about learning Polish to earn a living. But I do not even need French. My language is the sword's which every man understands. Yes, both the French and English have understood it.

That is fine, high-sounding prose but not in the least stilted, affected or needlessly brocaded. Though not colloquial, the speech is redeemed by a shy wit the sparkle and salt of which keep it surprisingly fresh for the reader. In fact, the virtues of this or any other passage of Reznikoff's work are the ones which can be found throughout it. It is consistent in its quality, and the achievement deserves to be known and valued. There was always an almost Olympian detachment about Reznikoff which must have been grounded in a profound conviction that in the long run a writer's rewards cannot help but be consonant with his desert.

Ernest Hemingway said in 1929, when *Farewell to Arms* was published, that for the first ten years after the Great War he had found the thought of the experience too painful to write about. Suffering may be the most moving of our memories, but for that very reason perhaps it is the most difficult to confront with complete aesthetic integrity. Reznikoff waited nearly thirty years before attempting to communicate in its entirety what the Holocaust had meant to him. As an American Jew, of course, he had no direct visceral contact with it like Elie Wiesel but had to attempt to recapture it imaginatively from afar like Bellow in *Mr. Sammler's Planet.* Yet this alone cannot completely account for the delay. The deepest reason must be sought elsewhere. Mary McCarthy once observed that the explosion of the atom bomb at Hiroshima "had made a hole in human history." The metaphor may be even more appropriate as a description of the feelings of the Jewish writer about the effect of the Hitler death camps on his mind.

For a long time it seemed as if Reznikoff would never treat the subject directly at all. He had said to me so many times that his emotions about it had entered into the parts of *Testimony* he was working on in the 1960s that I was taken by surprise when a portion of an unpublished manuscript entitled "Holocaust" and dated 1973 appeared as the concluding section of the volume *By the Well of Living and Seeing,* published in 1974. Until this time I had attributed his refusal to treat the forbidding subject directly to his aesthetic tact, his literary instinct that the explosive power of such a subject could hardly be contained, certainly not by someone who had not actually "been there." If even the expressions of survivors sometimes seemed to be little better than exploitative "kitsch" and those of others more sincere and genuine proved repetitive, diminishing and sentimental, was it possible for an American Jew to do any better? There was an abyss of cliché, propaganda and editorialism in the subject which even the wariest writer might have difficulty in avoiding. Was it possible, then, that the central event of Jewish history in almost two thousand years defied the imagination and had best be surrounded by silence? A poet might well be excused if he heeded the admonition of Emily Dickinson:

> Tell all the Truth but tell it slant—
> Success in Circuit lies . . .

The "circuit" that Reznikoff had found for his own emotions about the Holocaust seemed to lead through the landscape of terror and cruelty which (despite occasional comic relief) is the prevailing one of his *Testimony*. It seems, at any rate, that he himself thought so until the approach of his eightieth birthday. Then he apparently had a change of heart and decided otherwise.

Holocaust when it was published in its entirety in 1975, not long before its writer's death, proved to be anything but an anticlimax. It was clearly upon first reading a superior work of art (bearing in mind Pound's ironic caution in *Mauberley* that "no one knows, at sight, a masterpiece"), but just as clearly the precise reasons for its superiority, like those of a moving lyric, were elusive and did not permit much "purchase" for the reader attempting to analyze his impressions critically. In fact, from the point of view of textual explication, the absolute structural simplicity of *Holocaust* made it one of the most challenging and difficult works of our time—in its own way, in this respect at least, comparable to Pound's *Cantos*, Joyce's *Finnegans Wake* and Stein's *The Making of Americans*. Like these famous works, *Holocaust* exists, to be sure; it is *there* in somewhat the sense that the Great Pyramid is there. But what does it mean? What is one expected to say or do about this pyramid of skulls?

Describing *Holocaust* is a task. One difference between it and its predecessor *Testimony* is the complete absence of proper names from *Holocaust*. In *Testimony* the incidents and experiences reported are those of individuals (though the names used, as an author's note informs us, have been changed from the originals). But in *Holocaust* there are no names of persons, with the possible exception of Hitler (a name, however, which in the repeated expression "Heil Hitler" appears to be less that of a single being than it is the title of an institution, like Pharoah or Czar). What was exceptional in *Testimony*—the suppression of the notion of personality in the experiences described—becomes the inflexible rule in *Holocaust*. In the section entitled "Research," for example, we read the lines:

> A number of Jews had to drink sea water only
> to find out how long they could stand it.
> In their torment
> they threw themselves on the mops and rags
> used by the hospital attendants
> and sucked the dirty water out of them
> to quench the thirst
> driving them mad.

Anonymity is unusual but occasionally present in the earliest version of *Testimony*, published in 1934 with an Introduction by Kenneth Burke. It is also rare in *Testimony: The United States, 1885-1890*, published in 1965, in which one of the sections drawn from law reports of the South and entitled "Boys and Girls" contains the following little "vignette":

> The child was about eight years old.
> For some misconduct or other,
> his father stripped him naked, threw him on the floor,
> and beat him with a piece of rubber pipe,
> crying, "Die, God damn you!"
> He tried to dash the child against the brick surface of
> the chimney,
> and flung the child again heavily on the floor
> and stamped on him.

In the earlier work such selections are juxtaposed to others in which the persons are given proper names, even if these are only made-up ones. Something in the human imagination seems to require a name for the full assimilation of an experience. When a poet sees a flower, he is not satisfied, has not really completed his experience until he learns what it is called. He may even be looked upon as the bestower of names or at least as the transmitter of them. Primitive poems are full of names, lists of names (almost, it has been said, like telephone directories), and so are the most sophisticated and latest examples of the art: Homer, the Bible, but also Dante, Milton, Whitman and Pound. But in Reznikoff's *Holocaust,* all the names have vanished; what is left is abstraction (using the word in the sense Schopenhauer does when he observes: "Nations are really mere abstractions; individuals alone actually exist.").

There is another difference worth noting between *Testimony* and *Holocaust. Testimony,* from the 1930's through the 1960's, had been preceded by a striking epigraph, while *Holocaust* comes to us without any such clue. The epigraph has gone the way of the proper names. Now an epigraph is something more than merely decorative. It may be a sort of skeleton key which the writer has slipped under the doormat at the entryway of his work out of consideration for the reader who seeks admission into his intended meaning or the proper approach to that meaning. At the end of his career evidently Reznikoff had decided that such help, key or clue was no longer needed or else that it was not likely to be much use anyway. The epigraph of *Testimony* had apparently only puzzled some of its readers. The epigraph was a verse from the fourth chapter of Paul's *Epistle to the Ephesians*: "Let all bitterness and wrath, and anger, and clamor and railing, be put away from you with all malice." That is the 31st verse, and Reznikoff stops with it, but perhaps we may learn more about what he means by going on to the beginning of the following verse: "And be ye kind to one another, tender hearted, forgiving one another. . . ."

If any single set of words could sum up what animated Reznikoff, as I saw him, this would serve. But not all readers apparently agreed or saw it that way. Hayden Carruth, who had greeted Reznikoff's selected poems in the pages of the *Nation* with an extraordinary display of unaffected cordiality and enthusiasm in 1962, balked at accepting *Testimony* when it appeared in 1965. He seems to have interpreted the epigraph from the Gospel as Reznikoff's ironic mockery of so-called Christian civilization as it manifested itself in the United States during the period described in the book: the latter decades of the nineteenth century. He could see nothing but condemnation of America in the contrast between the sentiment of the Apostle and the brutal realities, mindless violence and cruelty depicted in the pages of the book. Back in 1934, Kenneth Burke had instead chosen to extol Reznikoff's compassion: "His bare presentation of the records places us before people who appear in the meager simplicity of their complaints. . . . One is made to feel very sorry for them, a humane response which far too much of our contemporary literature has neglected. . . ." Carruth, who was anything but insensitive to Reznikoff's poetic power and originality elsewhere, could not see this at all. He seems to have *under*read the meaning of epigraph and text in *Testimony,* while Burke may have *over*read it. In retrospect, it appears to be at least arguable that the balanced contrast of epigraph and text pointed in the direction of the philosophical attitude of Spinoza: "neither to laugh nor to cry" but unblinkingly to confront reality ("things as they are") and try to understand or, if not that, to understand that full understanding may be too much to expect from a mere creature like man. In a little book, *Jerusalem, the Golden,* published in 1934, the same year that saw the initial version of *Testimony,* Reznikoff had included a poem which he called "Spinoza":

> He is the stars,
> multitudinous as the drops of rain,
> and the worm at our feet,
> leaving only a blot on the stone;
> except God there is nothing.
>
> God neither hates nor loves, has neither pleasure nor pain;
> were God to hate or love, He would not be God;
> He is not a hero to fight our enemies,
> nor like a king to be angry or pleased at us,
> nor even a father to give us our daily bread, forgive our
> trespasses;
> nothing is but as He wishes,
> nothing was but as He willed it;
> as He wills it, so it will be.

Imitatio dei may be the ideal, but the closest approach to it possible for a human being may be the one stated in Dr. Aziz's memorable formula in Forster's *Passage to India:* "Kindness, more kindness, and even after that more kindness. . . . It is the only hope. . . ." Which is perhaps another way of saying what was said in the verse chosen by Reznikoff for his epigraph.

But Utopian dreaming and sentimental wish-fulfillment will not do as a substitute for real *charity*. The poem which follows the one on Spinoza in *Jerusalem, the Golden* is entitled "Karl Marx":

> We shall arise while the stars are still shining,
> while the street-lights burn brightly in the dawn,
> to begin the work we delight in,
> and no one shall tell us, Go,
> you must go now
> to the shop or office you work in
> to waste your life for your living.
> There shall be no more war, no more hatred;
> none of us shall die of sickness;
> there shall be bread and no one hunger for bread—
> and fruit better than any a wild tree grew.
> Wheels of steel and pistons of steel
> shall fetch us water and hew us wood;
> we shall call nothing mine—nothing for ourselves only.
> Proclaim to the seed of man
> throughout the length and breadth of the continents,
> From each according to his strength,
> to each according to his need.

This does not sound unsympathetic on first hearing, any more than his poem "The Socialists of Vienna," published in 1936 in *Separate Way* and celebrating the vain resistance by Austrian workers against suppression by their government in 1934, was unsympathetic to them. But are there not lines in this poem on Marx ("none of us shall die of sickness . . . we shall call nothing mine—nothing for ourselves only") which, like the starry-eyed idealism of Gonzalo's Utopian vision in *The Tempest* (a speech based by Shakespeare apparently on a passage in Montaigne's essay "Of Cannibals"—Gonzalo himself being an honest courtier who resembles Montaigne), seem gently to chide and question those who indulge in reveries that reconstruct the known facts about human nature and the human situation in the image of their own heart's desire? C. P. Snow may be going too far in one of the adjectives he uses to describe Reznikoff in the Introduction he wrote for *By the Waters of Manhattan*: "He is a deep, *sarcastic*, lonely writer," but one can sympathize with a reader who mistakes the complete detachment and impersonality of Reznikoff for a stronger form of irony than is really there. One must grant, too, that there are times in Reznikoff's poetry when the vigor of his reaction to a particular event makes it understandable why he should have chosen, for both *Jerusalem, the Golden* and the volume of his selected poems, *By the Waters of Manhattan*, an epigraph from Martial. The following is an example of work in his most savage mood:

> I remember very well when I asked you—
> as if you were a friend—whether or not
> I should go somewhere or other,
> you answered: "It does not matter:
> you are not at all important."
>
> That was true. But I wonder
> whom you thought important.
> Him who has been in his grave
> these ten years or more?
> He is not important now.
> Or him who is wearing out a path
> in the carpet of his room
> as he paces it
> like a shabby coyote in a cage,
> an old man hopelessly mad?
>
> Yourself, no doubt:
> looking like one
> who has been a great beauty.

To return to *Holocaust*, it is interesting to consider its beginning, which was a statement originally put into the mouth of a "narrator" and later reduced to a simple footnote on the opening page: "The National Socialist German Workers Party, known as the Nazis, took over Germany in January 1933. Their policy at first was merely to force the Jews to emigrate."

Reading these words, one wonders to whom they are being addressed. It sounds very much as if they were meant for the person to whom they brought news, and they serve to remind the contemporary reader, therefore, that, difficult as it may be for him to imagine it, things which he feels certain will be remembered forever will sooner or later be completely snowed under in the endless successions of time until "unforgettable" events have themselves become ancient history which only a few scholars will keep any record of.

When I began to reflect on the meaning and implications of that curious footnote I was eventually reminded of a passage in Céline's *Journey to the End of the Night.* The picaresque "hero" of that "epic" Ferdinand Bardamu, has had his mind almost destroyed by another historical "holocaust," World War I (in which 2,000,000 Frenchmen died and in which the author himself was badly wounded in the head), and he had chosen to seek refuge in an asylum from the lunacy of the bellicose "normal" world in which he feels he has been trapped. His romantic American sweetheart Lola cannot comprehend what she takes to be unpardonable cowardice on the part of her lover, whereupon he launches into an eloquent Falstaffian explanation of his dereliction of his soldierly duty:

> "Look, Lola, can you remember the name of any one of the soldiers who were killed in the Hundred Years War? Have you ever tried to find out one single name among them all? No, you can't, you've never tried, have you? To you, they're all anonymous, unknown and less important than the least atom in this paper weight on the table in front of you, less important than the food your bowels digested yesterday. You can see that they died for nothing. For nothing at all, the idiots. I swear that's true; you can see that it is. Only life itself is of any importance. Ten thousand years hence I bet you that this war, all important as it is now, will be completely forgotten. Possibly a dozen or so learned men may wrangle about it occasionally and about the dates of the chief hecatombs for which it was famous. Up to the present time that is all that Humanity ever succeeded in finding memorable about itself, after a few centuries have gone by, or a few years, or even after a few hours . . . I don't believe in the future, Lola . . ."

Cynicism such as this is, of course, far from being the whole truth, but there is enough truth in it to make it salutary as an antidote for the young idealist and romantic. Detached, standing by itself, the poltroonery of Falstaff (or that of Rabelais's Panurge) is as unbalanced as the heroics of Hotspur, but Céline delights in reminding us of melancholy truths that poets like Villon have never forgotten. The poet is the man for whom, paradoxically, time (like Joshua's sun) stands still, and for whom the snows of yesteryear disappear into oblivion along with everything upon which they fell. The one thing that never changes is that everything changes; everything is transitory and ephemeral and vain. That may be the inescapable fact that lies back of all the simultaneities and "montages" of Eliot's *Waste Land* and Pound's *Cantos,* where classical languages and modern ones, argot and jazz mingle without incongruity or confusion, and where Confucius, Augustine, Buddha, and Biblical prophets confront historical characters and our own contemporaries as naturally and with as much ease as some of them once did in Dante's supernatural Comedy.

Erudition of this sort, however, is far from the anonymity and language of *Holocaust.* The language is characterized by the kind of daylight clarity that Reznikoff seems to have dreamed of ever since he had been in law school:

> I felt no regret for the glittering words I had played with
> and the only pleasure to be working with ideas—
> of rights and wrongs and their elements
> and of justice between men in their intricate affairs . . .

The kind of style this impulse helped to create may be said to correspond somewhat perhaps to the one developed by the nineteenth-century American painter of pure "objects," William Harnett, who lived from 1848 to 1892.

From one point of view, the whole of Reznikoff's long artistic life may be regarded as a preparation to cope with the challenge of such a subject as the Holocaust. In an interview in 1969 with Professor L. S. Dembo at the University of Wisconsin, Reznikoff summed up his artistic credo by quoting a Chinese poet of the eleventh century whom he had read in a translation by A. C. Graham: "Poetry presents the thing in order to convey the feeling. It should be precise about the thing and reticent about the feeling." Graham himself glossed this in more familiar western terms when he said, "A rigor in seeking the objective correlative of emotion is a strong point of most Chinese poetry of all periods." Reznikoff quotes these passages with approval in 1969, but the same attitude may have been implicit in something he had said thirty-five years earlier, which was quoted by Kenneth Burke in the Introduction he wrote to *Testimony* in 1934:

> A few years ago, I was working for a publisher of law books, reading cases from every state and every year (since the country had become a nation). Once in a while I could see in the facts of a case details of the time and place, and it seemed to me that out of such material the century and a half during which the United States has been a nation could be written up, not from the standpoint of an individual, as in diaries, nor merely from the angle of the unusual, as in newspapers, but from every standpoint—as many standpoints as were provided by the witnesses themselves.

In the 1969 interview, he elaborated on what it meant to be a witness and the connection that existed in his mind between the concepts of witness and of poetry:

> I see something and it moves me and I put it down as I see it. In the treatment of it, I abstain from comment. Now, if I've done something that moves me—if I've portrayed the object well—somebody will come along and also be moved, and someone else will come along and say, "What the devil is this?" and maybe they're both right. But what I've written here will perhaps answer your question more directly: "By the term *objectivist* I suppose a writer may be meant who does not write directly about his feelings but about what he sees and hears; who is restricted almost to the testimony of a witness in a court of law; and who expresses his feelings indirectly by the selection of subject matter and, if he writes in verse, by its music." Now suppose in a court of law you are testifying in a negligence case. You cannot get up on the stand and

> say, "The man was negligent." That's a conclusion of fact. What you'd be compelled to say is how the man acted. Did he stop before he crossed the street? Did he look? The judges of whether he is negligent or not are the jury in the case and the judges of what you say as a poet are the readers. That is, there is an analogy between testimony in courts and the testimony of a poet.

The detachment achieved by Reznikoff and his refusal to write what may be described as "lachrymatory poetry" in *Holocaust* or to sit in judgment in any obvious way upon the devastating facts presented seem analogous to my mind to the coolness of Tolstoy in *War and Peace* when he sets aside his own feelings about the atrocities he depicts as the irrelevant results of prejudice and patriotism which must be discounted from a higher philosophical point of view. Tolstoy's attitude to his own human limitations produces one of the most thought-provoking passages in the whole book:

> It is impossible to say of the careers of Alexander and of Napoleon that they were beneficial or harmful, seeing that we cannot say wherein the benefit or harm of humanity lies. If anyone dislikes the career of either, he only dislikes it from its incompatibility with his own limited conception of what is for the good of humanity. Even though I regard as good the preservation of my father's house in Moscow in 1812, or the glory of the Russian army, or the flourishing of the Petersburg or some other university, or the independence of Poland, or the supremacy of Russia, or the balance of European power, or a special branch of European enlightenment—progress—yet I am bound to admit that the activity of any historical personage had, apart from such ends, other ends more general and beyond my grasp.

If such self-denial is genuine and not simply affected or a mere show of humility, it may be the hallmark of the rarest sort of intellectual probity and could provide the condition suitable to the creation of a work of art of such absolute transparency that it may strike some of its beholders as completely artless.

But how is one to know if seeming artlessness is indeed art of the highest order and that one is not being misled by one's own eager imagination? There are certain tests we can apply. There is, for example, the matter of just proportion, symmetrical balance, juxtaposition and contrast in the composition, which could not be there if its production was the result of mere chance. How striking it is, for example, that within a single page of each other (61 and 62 of *Holocaust)* we should find two such sharply contrasting pictures as, first, this:

> When the train on which the old doctor who had been
> a colonel in the Austrian army
> came to the death camp,
> he showed his diplomas
> and pictures of himself as a colonel;
> but this did not save him.
> The S.S. men beat him until he died
> and tore up his diplomas.

and, turning the page, this:

> Among the S.S. men there were exceptions.
> Some of the Jews in that camp
> were working at laying a narrow-gauge railroad
> to be used for carting bodies;
> and the man in charge would kill with his hammer.
> But one day there was another man in charge.
> Much as those working were afraid of the S.S.,
> a new man might be worse;
> and when they saw a new man, a senior officer at that,
> they were, to say the least, uneasy.
> One of the Jews had loaded sections of rail on his back
> and the new S.S. man said: "Why do you take so many?"
> So the Jew took off one
> but the S.S. man had him take off a few and said:
> "There's time. Walk slowly."
> The Jews saw him when the transports came—
> walking about and looking ashamed.
> Sometimes he would say a kind word to them.
> But he only stayed a month;

one evening he came into their barracks and said:
"I didn't know where I was being sent to.
I didn't know about this,
and when I found out I asked at once for a transfer.
I am leaving you now,"
and he shook hands with some of the Jews
and wished them to survive.

Does the second picture cancel out the meaning of the first or compensate for it? And if not, is it totally without meaning, since the first picture is much more statistically represenative of the experience of the death camps as it comes through the testimony selected by Reznikoff? The exception, we say, proves the rule; in other words, it both tests and confirms it. But the test may not be without meaning. Does it mean, then, that the world depicted is a world of chance meaninglessness, emptiness, even absurdity (to use a once fashionable term)? In any case, the kind S.S. man stands out in the darkness like a spot of light, a piece of gold that "gathers the light against it" in the prevailing gloom. The effect is a kind of moral chiaroscuro. The light is not to be forgotten, especially when it is so definite and insistent. Moses saw the heartless Egyptian overseer tormenting an Israelite, and his outrage prompted him to slay the Egyptian. The poet, amid all of the terrible brutality which he chronicles, observes an exceptional Nazi who, if any single person could do it, might revive one's faith in the possibility that human brotherhood is more than a flattering wish-fulfillment and an illusion. The last word in *Holocaust* is something of a victory for mercy, though it is presented as an incomplete and somewhat pitiful triumph:

Fishing boats, excursion boats, and any kind of boat
were mustered at the ports;
and the Jews were escorted to the coast by the Danes—
many of them students—
and ferried to safety in Sweden;
about six thousand Danish Jews were rescued
and only a few hundred captured by the Germans.

What are we to make of all this? Is it time to put all this sad history behind us by a conscious act of oblivion, if we can possibly manage it? Or must we learn from the tragic past, as the philosopher warned us to do, lest we repeat it? Or are we expected to learn that, whatever we choose to do about it, we cannot help being condemned to repeat it, either actually or imaginatively?

In his 1969 interview at the University of Wisconsin, Reznikoff spoke briefly about the reception accorded to his book *Testimony: The United States, 1885-1890* four years earlier. Despite a considerable publicity effort on the part of New Directions and its associate in the venture, the San Francisco Review, the book had never really managed to get off the ground. The author remembered one thing that had been said about his book: "A reviewer wrote that when he read *Testimony* a second time he saw a world of horror and violence. I didn't invent the world, but I felt it." In other words, the poet had done his work when he was simply truthful and had borne witness (perhaps in the sense of the word—going beyond the comparison to the courtroom made by Reznikoff himself—in which it is related etymologically to the Greek origin of the word *martyr)*. Reznikoff's remark reminds me somehow of Céline's report of his publisher Denoel's description of the manuscript of his novel *Guignol's Band*: "All I see in your book is brawling!" Céline's comment: "What does he see in existence?"

Writers like that seem to regard their work as performing a cathartic function for themselves and possibly for others, helping them somewhat to endure an otherwise unendurable reality. The poet Michael Heller, soon after the death of Reznikoff, began to worry *Holocaust* pertinaciously in an effort to pin down its intention precisely. His conclusion is that "these poems in their sheer factualness command response but do not dictate it. The author gives both good and bad conscience their due. This, of course, is a modernity with a vengeance." He may have had in mind a passage such as the following:

> We are the civilized
> Aryans;
> and do not always kill those condemned to death
> merely because they are Jews
> as the less civilized might:
> we use them to benefit science
> like rats or mice . . .

Or a footnote on page 40: ". . . Whatever the method of execution it was, to quote an official report, 'always honorable and done in a humane and military manner.' "

Or the footnote on page 111 with which *Holocaust* concludes (a kind of postscript which follows the account of the Danish rescue):

> The uprising of the Jews in the Warsaw Ghetto began in the spring of 1943 and lasted about twenty days. Of the thousands of Jews still in the ghetto when the uprising began perhaps a few hundred escaped alive. A greater number were killed by the blowing up of their dugouts and the sewers. But, despite the burden on every S.S. man and German police officer during the actions to drive out the Jews from Warsaw—where they had once numbered a quarter of a million—the spirit of the S.S. men and the police officers, it was noted by one of their superiors, was "extraordinarily good and praiseworthy from the first day to the very last."

What caught Reznikoff's attention may have been something that Maurice Samuel speaks of in his own way in a passage of his 1968 book *Light on Israel*:

> The word genocide was coined to express the uniqueness of Germany's crime against the Jews and much has been written concerning the beastliness with which it was carried out. But genocide is no new thing. Peoples have been destroyed before so that their territories might be occupied, and the Jews were not the only ones towards whom the Germans harbored genocidal intentions. Revolting cruelties, too, are a familiar feature of human history. The peculiarity of Germany's superbly organized extermination of the Jews was its idealism, its practical pointlessness. A complicated and exacting industry of death was created at a high cost to the war effort. . . . The German leaders and the tens of thousands who worked with such a will at the unnatural business were convinced that the destruction of the Jews served a high principle which for some transcended the welfare of the Vaterland itself. . . .

Reznikoff might add, however, that you can't argue with history and can therefore hardly describe the "business" as unnatural. For how can you know what is natural to humanity until you face what it is capable of doing? In Jewish apologetics, a Jewish historian of the seventeenth century is often quoted as saying that he would draw a veil of silence around the worst of the atrocities and abominations committed against the Jews during the Chmielnicki Cossack massacres "lest we bring shame upon the image of man himself." That may be a praiseworthy sentiment, but it does not correspond to Reznikoff's. The historical record is precisely what he does not wish to shy away from. At the same time, he refuses to exaggerate or to deny the bright spots of human nature which serve sometimes to relieve the darkness of the picture. A passage from Louis Simpson's *Three on a Tower* may be applicable perhaps as a description of Reznikoff's approach: "The Romantics expressed their emotions. The Symbolist poets dreamed. An age of science demanded the poet of facts." Such an approach, stressing the decisive authority of experience itself, though new in terms of the self-consciousness with which it is adopted by some twentieth-century poets, may have been present in some earlier American writers. Emily Dickinson (a poet whose brevity, concentration and resolute refusal of sentimentality Reznikoff found to his own taste) expressed the attitude in a characteristic way a century ago:

> Experience is the Angled Road
> Preferred against the Mind
> By—Paradox—the Mind itself—
> Presuming it to lead
>
> Quite opposite—how complicate
> The Discipline of Man—
> Compelling him to choose Himself
> His Preappointed Pain—

Experience, of course, must be understood to include not only everything one sees or feels directly but everything one hears or reads about as well. It includes, too, everything we are capable of imagining and which is not simply "lost upon us."

"Sincerity" was almost the first word used to describe the impression of Reznikoff's work by Louis Zukofsky in the Objectivist issue of *Poetry* in 1931. It may be the last word to be said as well. But what is this quality of "sincerity"? T. S. Eliot has one suggestion in the Preface he wrote for Charles Louis Philippe's little novel *Bubu de Montparnasse*:

> Philippe's great quality is not imagination: it is a sincerity which makes him a faithful recorder of things as they are, and of events as they happened, without irrelevant and disturbing comment. He had a gift which is rare enough: the ability not to think, not to generalize. To be able to select, out of personal experience, what is really significant, to be able not to corrupt it by afterthoughts, is as rare as imaginative invention. I am always impressed in Philippe by his fidelity to the powers that were given him; nearly always . . . he is saying what he has to say, not writing a book. He was not *un homme de lettres.*

Whatever one may say, a writer like Reznikoff will continue to be problematical for some readers. His editorial silences and extreme reticence make him so. If comment can be disturbing, as Eliot says, refusal to comment at all may be equally disturbing. It is instructive perhaps to compare Reznikoff in this respect with Walt Whitman and Gertrude Stein. Whitman tried to grasp the nature of the difficulty he presented to readers when he wrote in a late preface to his *Leaves,* "A Backward Glance O'er Travelled Roads": "The word I myself put primarily for the description of the *Leaves* . . . is the word *suggestiveness.* I round out and finish little, if anything. . . . The reader will always have his or her part to do, just as much as I have mine." On another occasion he remarked: "Not the book needs so much to be the complete thing. But the reader of the book does." One day he said to his young friend Horace Traubel: "It has often occurred to me that perhaps all through the poems I assume too largely the responding sympathetic gifts of the reader."

But it is just these gifts that enable some readers to guide others, to open their eyes, ears, hearts, or if not that at least to arrest their attention and persuade them that they might be missing something for lack of sufficient sensitivity in the organ necessary for its reception. Such gifts do not seem widely distributed; to many they are denied altogether. They do not necessarily accompany intelligence, and even the highest intelligence may be useless for perception without them. Robert Louis Stevenson knew this when, after recommending *Leaves of Grass* in the most extravagant terms, he added the caution: "But it is only a book for those who have the gift of reading." For me, the nature of this gift is hinted at in a passage of "Song of Myself" which has itself puzzled (as I myself have seen) otherwise clever readers: "He who walks a furlong without sympathy walks to his own funeral dressed in his shroud." (You may find this sentiment revolting, as D. H. Lawrence did when he "answered" Whitman with the witticism: "Hats off! My funeral is passing by!" but that is the reaction of one who understands Whitman only too well and does not draw the complete blank that some readers apparently do.) My own feeling is that, to paraphrase Whitman, whoever reads a page of Whitman, Stein or Reznikoff without sharing the thought, sentiment, and sympathetic *attention* that have gone into the writing will never grasp its import and will have wasted his time.

The question has been raised with regard to such works as *Testimony* and *Holocaust* about whether they should be classified as works of art at all. How do they differ—except for being much less voluminous—from the original and difficult documents upon which they are based, the law reports of the various states of the union and the testimony in the Nuremberg war crimes trials? How, for that matter, do they differ from such documentary dramas, based in large part on the same sources, as those of Peter Weiss (e.g., *The Investigation*)? Are they not still essentially raw material awaiting the magical metamorphosis of art rather than art itself? What distinguishes them from that collection of fifteen actual case histories, which, we are told, Dreiser collected into a scrapbook which he called "American Tragedies" and which served as the material for his great unified fictional transmutation in *An American Tragedy* (though the changes are often minimal ones from the actual newspaper reports upon which he drew for the factual background of his novel)?

The answers to these questions could be grouped under the headings of *selection, style* and *understatement*. From the descriptive examples of Dreiser's documentary "American Tragedies," cited by his wife Helen in her book about him, it is clear —as it is from Dreiser's own poems in *Moods, Cadenced & Declaimed*—that he had little of Reznikoff's delicate feeling for English words, their resonances, overtones, image-creating potential or the way they might be combined into clear, pleasing patterns. As for the comparison with Peter Weiss, it seems to me far afield if only because Reznikoff so stubbornly eschews all obvious drama as well as melodrama, flattens it all out and reduces the color contrasts to a monochromatic effect that is an almost uniform Corot-type of gray. This restraint was noticed in him from the outset of his career and even by his most sympathetic critics was regarded with some suspicion as bordering nearly upon affectation: "At times," wrote Kenneth Burke in 1934 of *Testimony*, "his 'objective' recital becomes a bit too artful in its understatement." Some might even see in the extreme to which he carries this latter-day Anglo-Saxon quality a trait which marks him as a Jew separated by only a few years from immigrant parents who came from a Slavic background in which emotional expression and even self-indulgence were acceptable modes of behavior. Though Gertrude Stein's family was German-Jewish rather than East European, some of her literary characteristics, which gave her an air so extremely "modern," may also be traced possibly to an analogous reaction against some of the emotionalism familiar to her in childhood.

Dreiser secured his effects through a massively and minutely realistic technique which has been well-described as aiming at "saturation." Reznikoff, on the other hand, is strictly selective and cuts away irrelevant detail as much as possible, though he aims, through his selectivity, to create what the poet Yeats described as "an emotion of multitude." In stressing the difference, I do not mean to suggest that Dreiser's work, especially in some of his prose—I put aside his verse and drama—is ineffectual. Quite the contrary. He has always been one of my favorite writers. His laborious accumulations of detail and the emotion with which he is able to infuse them constitute a kind of lyricism that has always stirred me deeply. His depictions of the American scene of his time are paintings (as distinguished from photographs) which have great subjective aesthetic power, and he will always rank not only as a great American writer among his contemporaries but as one of the great writers in all of American literary history. Yet his gift is of another kind than Reznikoff's; he seems to succeed in moving the reader almost in spite of the awkwardness of his language, which gets in his way more often than it comes to his aid. Reznikoff's well-trained words, on the other hand, always obey him, and becoming aware of this is a pleasure he offers his reader. He is, to be sure, no sensuous stylist in the Romantic manner of Keats as Scott Fitzgerald is. His painting surfaces are harder, more opaque, more "photographic" if you like, though I myself would not choose to describe him so. He resembles, as I have already indicated, at least in some respects, the quality achieved by a nineteenth-century "objectivist" painter like William Harnett. I do not know if the term *objectivist* has ever been applied to Harnett's work, but it would certainly seem to me to be not only applicable but apt as a description.

I'd like to try to answer, in other ways than I may have already done, three questions about *Holocaust* (which are also applicable to *Testimony*):

What does it mean?

The question might be approached indirectly by way of further exploring the meaning of Objectivism. Objectivism is taken to be what W. C. Williams had in mind when he wrote his well-known line in *Paterson*: "No ideas but in things." What lies back of this formulation I take to be similar to Pound's thought: "The natural object is always the adequate symbol."

Reznikoff himself said: "I believe in writing about the object itself, and I let the reader, or listener, draw his own conclusions. . . ." He commended to his listeners an expression of an attitude cultivated by *Zen*, which inspired certain forms of Japanese art: "forgetfulness of self." This attitude was connected in his mind with what he strove, as a writer, both to learn and to teach: "the lesson of objectivity."

He was skeptical of all frills and ornamentation, even those which are generally regarded not only as proper to poetry but as perhaps essential to it. Though he could create memorable images, he aspired to dispense with the need of them, quite as his iconoclastic ancestors did. A passage in some notes he once made for a talk is worth repeating:

With respect to direct speech: (Incidentally, I remember how annoyed my instructor in the law of equity was with the expression common in law cases, the plaintiff must come into equity "with clean hands." He objected to "with clean hands" because it was a metaphor.) I found the following in a review of two translations of Sappho in *The New York Review of Books* (March 3, 1966) not without interest: "At her most intense she writes the kind of poetry Stevens dreamed of, a poetry that 'without evasion by a single metaphor' sees 'the very thing itself and nothing else.' English poetry is, in this special sense, incurably 'evasive' and requires a richer medium to achieve equally powerful effects."

In *Testimony* and *Holocaust* he managed to rid himself almost completely of figurative language and embellishments, and the numerous revisions to which he subjected the manuscripts of these poems were chiefly designed to cleanse them of all incidental imagery which was "immaterial and irrelevant." His development reminds us that poetry may refresh and refurbish the language in two ways: by introducing original metaphors or by eliminating worn-out ones. In the early part of his life Reznikoff concentrated upon the first; later, on the second.

A maximum of simplification (which, in the case of Gertrude Stein, has been called a kind of "art by subtraction") may unexpectedly result in a maximum of suggestiveness. It was Reznikoff's conviction that when objectification in art is completely successful, the comparisons, analogies, and interpretations which it suggests may be "sometimes better than the writer himself intended and profounder." He alluded to a Hindu saying that "a work of art has many faces."

What of the verse-form?

Reznikoff called it recitative. As a noun, the word *recitative* connotes freedom from strict form in tonal and metrical structure, rhetorical rather than melodic in its phrasing. According to the dictionary, it also implies a tone or rhythm peculiar to a language, dialect, or individual author's style. As an adjective, the word connects with the idea of narrative, rehearsal and repetition. To lovers of music, the word is tied firmly to the characteristic texture of oratorios, especially those of Bach and Handel. In fact, the musical associations of the word are its primary ones.

Reznikoff insisted on the importance of the musical element in poetry. He quoted with approval Pound's dictum that "poetry begins to decay when it gets too far from music." Reznikoff himself asserts that "the words move out of prose into verse as the speech becomes passionate and musical instead of flat."

But Reznikoff's taste was for music of a particular kind—he called it (beautifully enough) "a Doric music." The original meaning of the word *Doric* implied something unrefined, rustic, even uncouth. In English, it was, less than two centuries ago, an epithet of disdain. When critics spoke of "the Doric dialect" of the Lake Poets, they did not mean to flatter Wordsworth. But to Reznikoff, who credits Wordsworth even more than Whitman with the introduction into high poetic style of "the language of common speech," *Doric* was an adjective with attractive associations. The word, of course, is also a term in architecture. It is the name of the oldest and simplest of Greek orders, a column which was adopted in a modified form by the Romans. In printing, Doric is an old kind of type face, impressive in its simplicity of design. The various senses all point to an austere beauty.

The simplicity of Reznikoff's form is artful. It confronts the reader as something consciously old-fashioned. It is upright, unadorned, a little child-like and primitive in a manner which cannot be outmoded because it has never been modish. Reznikoff said: "I have read somewhere that among the ancient Greeks there was an intermediary between song and straight prose—I suppose that is chanted. A good deal of the Bible is read like that in the Orthodox service in synagogue."

Reznikoff recognized that his "square" form was likely to be as unfashionable as his quest for clarity in a time in which to be cryptic continued to be the fashion just as it had been in the time of the Symbolists, who held that "to name is to destroy."

In what way does Reznikoff make the material his own?

The words are his. Reznikoff's relation to his documentary sources may perhaps be compared to that of a translator to his text, and one may find a clue to the nature of his efforts in a quotation which he made from an essay by R. P. Blackmur on Pound as translator: "If the uses of language include expression, communication, and the clear exhibition of ideas, Mr. Pound is everywhere a master of his medium so long as the matter at hand is not his own . . . is translation or paraphrase."

There are three separate quite different manuscripts of *Holocaust* totalling well over one thousand pages, plus several lengthy manuscript fragments. These typescripts have been revised again and again by Reznikoff in his tiny holograph so as to be rendered almost undecipherable. These manuscript pages clearly reveal the writer's tireless struggle to simplify, to clarify, and to objectify. The first person singular is consistently replaced by the third person (singular or plural) or by proper nouns. Lines are rearranged or broken up into different lengths in search of sound more appropriate to the sense. Words not absolutely necessary are eliminated, occasionally at some risk of obscuring the meaning. A line which in the final text reads:

> and the man in charge would kill with his hammer

had earlier read:

> and the man in charge of us would kill people with his hammer.

Direct speech is trimmed down until what is left has an almost Biblical simplicity. Lines which were originally:

> "Why do you take so many of these?"
> "We have time . . . You can walk slowly."

eventually become:

> "Why do you take so many?"
> "There's time. Walk slowly."

"Strong" expressions are shaded toward understatement. "They were frightened" becomes "They were, to say the least, uneasy." Adjectives are pared down: "Very much ashamed" gives way to "much ashamed" and finally becomes simply "ashamed." Latinate or formal-sounding diction is replaced. "When I learned," in a speech, becomes the more colloquial "When I found out."

What seems like emphatic editorial comment—however legitimate—is toned down or dropped from the final version. The vignette of the exceptional, compassionate S.S. officer had been followed originally by the line: "But he was the only one like that." Eventually, the passage ends without this "framing" line. Since the passage had opened with the words: "Among the S.S. men there were exceptions" the repetition in the concluding line was not necessary. It merely underlined the obvious and did not trust the reader.

Bridge passages and specific dates and years are removed from the text in the interest of condensation or else they are put into notes at the bottom of the page. The drama is acted out, like the Bible's, against a backdrop of eternity. It could just as easily have all happened (except for the modern machinery and weapons) in medieval or in ancient times. It could happen in one place as well as in another. The scenes of *Testimony* unfold in the United States, those in *Holocaust* in eastern Europe, but the nature of man which has given rise to the situations in both is evidently the same.

Testimony grew out of a feeling for "found objects" of common life, and it came to Reznikoff apparently out of a job he held at the time it was written. A note appended to the original *Testimony* tells the reader. "All that follows is based on law reports of the several states. The names of all persons are fictitious and those of villages and towns have been changed." The circumstances in which the book was composed are probably the ones described in one of his lovely little lyrics:

> After I had worked all day at what I earn my living,
> I was tired. Now my work has lost another day,
> I thought, but began slowly,
> and slowly my strength came back to me.
> Surely the tide comes in twice a day.

In making a virtue of necessity, there is a suggestion here which is relevant to a world in which many people are compelled to do many things which do not in the least express themselves yet who must find an outlet for self-expression. It is a poem of encouragement to all the young whose energies are drained in the struggle to make a living but who are not so completely exhausted that they are not up to the task of creating or of "framing" things of aesthetic or intellectual merit and interest which may grow out of their working experience. What would modern art be without its amateurs, primitives, "Sunday painters," and those ladies whom Emerson once described as "portfolio poets"? Some of the best modern artists and writers, too, have been men and women of independent means, or else have found patrons who enabled them to resist the demands of the marketplace and to work entirely apart from it. In a general sense, Reznikoff, who was never rich, may be said to belong to this great modern tradition of those who refused to work for the market rather than for themselves.

Holocaust contrasts sharply with *Testimony* in that its sensational subject matter has been exploited by various forms of journalism and popular literature to a point of such triteness as to make it virtually unredeemable for the serious writer. If the problem in *Testimony* was to heighten the interest of the commonplace and ordinary, in *Holocaust* it is to subdue the melodramatic and unusual. The honesty, integrity and restraint of the result make it one of the few which will be tolerable or persuasive to temperaments like Reznikoff's own. It is a literary artifact which, in its homely simplicity of design and construction, seems well-made enough to be durable. In this respect it is like his other work. Nothing he ever did was hasty, shoddy or ill-done.

I remember reading somewhere that the trouble with the so-called Objectivists in America in the 1930's was that they all seemed to be "prematurely middle-aged." If that is true (I'm by no means sure it is) it may have been the result of their coming upon the literary scene at a particularly somber moment in American history—the onset of the Great Depression which followed the 1929 stock-market crash. Or it may have resulted in part from the fact that a quality then prized in some of the avant-garde literary circles (and especially by such men as T. S. Eliot and by his chosen mentor at Harvard, Irving Babbitt) was the quality of *maturity*. Words like *responsible* began once more to have an attractive sound in intellectual ears. The American "cult of youth" became increasingly the butt of irony and depreciation even among those writers (like Scott Fitzgerald) who exemplified it and were its culture-heroes. In *The Beautiful and Damned,* Fitzgerald speaks of America in a cutting tone of European contempt (which one might expect from a man like Pound) as "a continent that had been turned by its women into a gigantic nursery." Or else the premature "senility" of the Objectivists might have come from the fact that their leading figures (Zukofsky, Oppen, Rakosi, Reznikoff) were all Jewish.

Is it entirely accidental that one of the greatest writers of the twentieth century, the Triestan master Italo Svevo—whose admirers have included, among many others, Joyce, Eugenio Montale and Saul Bellow, and who was an assimilated Jew born (like Kafka) in the old Austro-Hungarian Empire with the name Ettore Schmitz—should have been obsessed from first to last with the theme which he himself called senility, premature senility? The significance of the possible connection between Jewishness and this theme did not occur to me, I confess, until I was recently reminded of an incident involving Pound related in the memoir by his daughter, who tells how her father took her one day to see the movie *Snow White* and sat through it twice because he liked it even more than she did. On another occasion, she tells how, after seeing a movie of Fred Astaire and Ginger Rogers, Babbo (as she calls Pound) danced through the streets all the way home, and, after reaching home, he went to his room, took off his coat, and continued "to leap and tap-dance" vigorously and uninhibitedly. Reading this reminiscence of Pound brought to my mind, in sharp contrast, a verse which Reznikoff had written in his *Rhythms II,* which he had printed privately in 1919 at the age of twenty-five and had entitled "Vaudeville":

> I leave the theater
> keeping step, keeping step to the music.
> It sticks to my feet,
> stepped into dung . . .

Even at that early age apparently, Reznikoff resented the hold that mindless frivolity exercises upon us. The spirit of gravity does not appear to be a pose. Of course, we see Pound's childlike delight through the eyes of a child. Reznikoff's verse might have been an afterthought, "emotion recollected in tranquility." But it is not insignificant nevertheless. Whoever has looked upon the faces of Jewish immigrant children, like the one in the photograph of Mary Antin and her sister which still serves as the frontispiece of her celebrated book *The Promised Land,* must be struck by the look of care and age imprinted there. Reznikoff himself was not an immigrant to the United States, but he is removed from that generation of immigrants like Mary Antin by a mere decade, and he recalled all his life the feelings of fear he experienced in early encounters with anti-Semitic violence in his neighborhood. In the verse from *Rhythms,* he shows himself responding instinctively to the dance-step of the vaudeville he has just seen, but he has only a feeling of disgust for the effect it has upon him. After all, as Einstein once observed, a man responding mechanically to a march played by a military band has no use for the great brain with which he was endowed by nature; his spinal column would be sufficient.

Is it possible that to be born a Jew—at least until very recently and in the shadow of the diaspora and all that followed—means to have been born old or at least to be more quickly aged than other children? It would be strange if it were otherwise. The historian Toynbee offended Jewish feelings when he spoke of Judaism as a fossil. He might have been on sounder ground had he spoken of Jews as exposed by their situation to early aging and "senility" before their time. For a long while, Jews for this very reason may have been "out of phase" with the rhythms of the world, but now, after Hiroshima and the Holocaust, the world itself may have suddenly aged and become, if not senile, at least sensible of its potential in that direction.

Perhaps something more should be said about the influence of Reznikoff's training in the law upon him as a poet, for it was considerable as we have seen, not only in supplying him with much of his material but in training him to examine and cross-examine words meticulously. Concerning the influence of William Carlos Williams's training in medicine upon his work, Randall Jarrell (in his Introduction to Williams's *Selected Poems*) has written: "Williams has the knowledge of people one expects, and often does not get, from doctors; a knowledge one does not expect, and almost never gets, from contemporary poets." He goes on to specify Eliot as one of the poets he has in mind. Louis Simpson, in his *Three on a Tower,* has this to add to Jarrell's observation: "His work as a doctor furnished him with characters and incidents. He recalls things he saw on his rounds, what people said, the accounts they gave of their lives. In this he resembles Whitman, who tended the sick during the Civil War." (It might make an interesting book if someone with literary sensibility were to discuss the influence that a training in medicine had upon writers like Rabelais, Chekhov, Maugham, Léon Daudet and Céline.)

It is clear, in retrospect, that, as was the case with William Carlos Williams, Reznikoff's real calling from the beginning was to be a writer and that he chose to prepare himself to enter one of the recognized traditional professions (his brother Paul Reznikoff became a physician who rose to an honored place in the profession) as a way of earning his living. Unlike Williams, however, he was never able to resist the impulse to write sufficiently long to consummate a commitment to practice law.

Three things might be said about the effect that contact with the study of American law had upon Reznikoff. First, it disciplined him to regard words skeptically and to examine statements by himself or others with scrupulous care. There are passages in his work—I am thinking of one in *Family Chronicle*—in which a moral question is discussed from all sides with what might be described as Talmudical subtlety. Such casuistry has its use for the sort of mastery of words that a poet like Reznikoff sets out to attain. This leads to a second observation. When T. S. Eliot made his familiar pronouncement that "the spirit killeth but the letter giveth life," he was not only turning a familiar expression upside down (like Oscar Wilde when he reversed Aristotle's doctrine by observing that "Life imitates art"); he was also pointing out to poets attempting to lift themselves, as he himself was doing, out of the slough of romantic, sentimental and uncritical sloppiness, that they must become more precise in their use of words. They should say exactly what they mean and not rely on the reader's good will and enthusiastic feeling of agreement to tide them over. It is just such a reserved manner of reading the meaning of agreements and contracts and attending carefully to testimony that the serious study of law inculcates. It is another way of learning how to exercise verbally the quality which Eliot's teacher Babbitt described with the Emersonian expression "the inner check."

Finally, the study of law cannot but help sharpen one's awareness of the gap separating law from justice, though ideally the two are supposed to coincide. Those who study the records of the law are hardly likely to equate naively law and justice. The whole question of the existence of absolute justice, which is not relative to particular circumstances and man-made rules, arises from the study of laws, a consideration of their historical backgrounds, and their applications to specific cases tried in the courts.

From the time of his earliest volume of *Testimony* (based on a concept in poetry so completely original that I cannot think of any precedent for it), Reznikoff seems to have been fascinated by the triumph of the forms of the law not only over justice but over the intent of the makers of the law and even over those who administer and argue about it. The coincidence of the verdicts handed down by the law and what abstract justice would seem to require appears to be nothing but—a coincidence.

The most problematical aspect of all is when the law itself is at odds with justice. The strenuous effort among those who administered the death camps was to preserve the appearance that things were done there in accordance with the dictates of German law. Yet all the while, there were indications that justice ultimately would not be cheated, even by the law. Reznikoff had some lines in an early poem which might be quoted here:

> Do not mourn the dandelions—
> that their golden heads become gray
> in no time at all
> and are blown about in the wind;
> each season shall bring them again to the lawns;
> but how long the seeds of justice
> stay underground
> how much blood and ashes of precious things
> to manure so rare and brief a growth.

It is ironic that those who cultivate tidy lawns are not always enthusiastic about the colorful wild flowers that appeal to the poet's eye and do their best to eradicate them. It is frustrating to them to find such uncultivated growths, since there seems to be something in nature ("deep down things" as Hopkins writes) which cares for every form of life no matter how unruly, and especially it may be said for life which has come to flower. Whitman moves us when he declares his love for the humblest "mossy scabs of the worm fence . . . elder, mullein and pokeweed." And Thoreau, in the same vein, beholds "in wildness the preservation of the world." Reznikoff thus has plenty of American and poetic precedent when he finds in the persistence of wild flowers which gardeners may behead but not completely destroy a metaphor for the stubborn survival of justice in this violent world, a faith which not every Jew in the wake of the Holocaust has found it easy to sustain.

Like many significant writers of the twentieth century, Reznikoff is concerned with Time, which provokes him to some piercing poetic utterances:

> Now the sky begins to turn upon its hub—
> the sun; each leaf revolves upon its stem;
>
> now the plague of watches and of clocks nicks away
> the day—
> ten thousand thousand steps
> tread upon the dawn;
> ten thousand wheels
> cross and criss-cross the day
> and leave their ruts across its brightness;
>
> the clocks
> drip
> in every room—
> our lives are leaking from the places,
> and the day's brightness dwindles into stars.

Yet time in the end seemed kind to him. In the last fifteen years of his life, increasing recognitions were coming to him in his own country and in England not simply as a Jewish poet writing in the English language but as an American poet.

He was busy with new publishing projects. He walked for miles each day through city streets and parks to the last. He was almost as old as Goethe. Death, when it came, was not sudden, but his suffering was mercifully brief (he had a heart seizure in the evening and died next morning). He left readers who had not known him personally and others who had known his kindness but had never read his poetry, mourning him with feeling. Having been "born old" or at least prematurely aged by his experience of a harsh world, he succeeded in reversing the order of time, so that it might be said of him that, at the age of eighty-one, he died young.

Milton Hindus is the author of many critical books, including *The Proustian Vision, A Reader's Guide to Marcel Proust, F. Scott Fitzgerald: An Introduction and Interpretation*, and *Walt Whitman: The Critical Heritage.* His *Leaves of Grass: One Hundred Years After* was awarded the Walt Whitman Prize by the Poetry Society of America in 1959. Since 1948 he has been at Brandeis University where he is now Professor of English, and he has contributed articles and reviews to such newspapers and magazines as *The New York Times Book Review, The New York Herald-Tribune Books, The Chicago Tribune* and *Atlantic Monthly.*

Printed April 1977 in Santa Barbara for the Black Sparrow Press by Mackintosh & Young. Design by Barbara Martin. This edition is published in paper wrappers & 400 copies have been handbound in boards by Emily Paine.